Other books in the Sufism Lecture Series:

Sufism

Sufism and Wisdom

Sufism and Knowledge

Sufism and Islam

Sufism and Peace

Molana Salaheddin Ali Nader Shah Angha
"Pir Oveyssi"

University of Göteborg
Peace and Development Research Institute

November 2, 1994

M.T.O. SHAHMAGHSOUDI® PUBLICATIONS

M.T.O. Shahmaghsoudi® Publications

Angha, Salaheddin Ali Nader Shah

Sufism and Peace

Copyright © 1996 by Maktab Tarighat Oveyssi Shahmaghsoudi *(School of Islamic Sufism)*.® All rights reserved — copyright throughout the world. No part of this publication may be reproduced, stored in a retrieval system, or transmitted in any form by any means without the express written consent of holder of copyright, the President of M.T.O. Shahmaghsoudi.

Library of Congress Catalog Card Number: 95-077988
ISBN: 0-910735-96-4

First edition: 1996
Second edition: 1997

Printed in the U.S.A.

Published and distributed by M.T.O. Shahmaghsoudi
5225 Wisconsin Ave., N.W. Suite #502
Washington, D.C. 20015
U.S.A.

website: http://mto.shahmaghsoudi.org

Contents

Introduction
page 1

Sufism and Peace
page 7

Geneaology of
Maktab Tarighat Oveyssi Shahmaghsoudi
(School of Islamic Sufism)®
page 23

Wherever the masculine gender is used, it is solely for the purpose of linguistic convenience. Since the intent of religion is for the spiritual elevation of each individual, we believe that religion addresses the soul, and the soul is not subject to gender classification.

Introduction

A few years ago Hazrat Pir began one of his lectures by asking the audience these questions, "If there were only one in the world, and that one were you, what would be your name? Who would you be? Would you hate? Would you love?" Only an instant lapsed before he calmly asked, "If there were one, and that one had all the knowledge of the universe, and could respond to all your needs and all your wants, what would you do?" Then he said, Sufism is about this "ONE".

Hazrat Pir's method of teaching is definitely thought provoking, and his students say demanding and challenging. Some say he evokes the same system of learning as Socrates did with his students. Those who have interviewed him usually confess that they are totally disarmed by his questions, becoming engaged in an intense learning experience. True to his mission, Hazrat Pir never ceases to teach. His main goal is to show people how they may attain the true state of human dignity, peace and tranquility. His definition of the human being rises above social, cultural and psychological definitions.

Sophisticated communication systems have linked people worldwide, breaking down the "absolutes" that societies, communities and countries had defined and kept sacred for themselves. It is the age of relativity. While exposure to diversity has expanded people's vision of the world, it has also brought elements of insecurity and instability into the day-to-day life of many people. When standards collapse and values shift, where can we find the ultimate definition of our "self"?

Hazrat Pir says, "Each person is a complex and unique masterpiece." Most people, if not all, would like this statement to be true. But what prevents us from experiencing it? What must happen for us to even understand the magnitude of this statement? If we don't allow our imagination to quickly define it, package it and file it away, we could start on a powerful journey of self-realization, which would change the entire fabric of societies, human interactions and legal and social systems. This means moving through the multidimensional patterns of social conditionings that have structured our lives, formed our identities, personalities, self-worth, our perceptions of others and our value systems.

How can we put these aside? And if we should put them aside what would be the yardstick with which we could measure our achievements, our knowledge and our understanding of anything?

Hazrat Pir says, "You are the measure for everything." He is often heard saying, "You have everything that you need. All you need to do is to lift the boundaries you have created, then 'reality' will unveil." But if one wants to be this "unique masterpiece", how, realistically, does one "lift the boundaries?"

"Know thyself," wrote the philosopher Plato about integrity; because "an unexamined life is not worth living." From the time of the Greeks, Western philosophy has advocated self-knowledge — internal learning. Internal learning is at the heart of Islam. As the Holy Prophet Muhammad has said, "Whoever knows the true self knows God."

To begin at the beginning — know thyself. The "i", the individual, is a cherished concept, the acknowledged foundation upon which democracy is built. By transforming the "i", one can go a long way towards transforming the greater world in which the "i" lives. The belief in the perfectibility of the Self has strengthened the fiber of Western society and the collapse of this belief in the twentieth century has brought about alienation and uncertainty in modern societies. Untouched by today's social, economic and political shifts, Hazrat Pir represents a strong and clear voice, reminding us of the urgency to know the true and stable "I". In so doing, he reaffirms the human being's capacity to master the self.

One of the significant contributions of Hazrat Pir to the reservoir of world knowledge is the idea that, because the world has projected its divisions and boundaries onto the vulnerable "i", one must create a process for achieving mastery of mind. This is done by first removing these divisions and boundaries onto the "i" through an inner experience of religion that begins with spiritual integration and ends with a complete metamorphosis. It is no coincidence that two of the healthiest and strongest mystical minds of the Catholic tradition — St. John of the Cross and St. Teresa of Avila — learned much about their mystical journey from Islam as it was received into the Spanish Moorish tradition.

Much can be learned from the way Hazrat Pir teaches. Ideally, a student should think: "I will commit myself not to the idea but the process of mastering my own mind and if enough of us do the same 'the world' will simultaneously change because 'the world' is us." A simple way of stating a complicated process, but it is a beginning.

This series of essays, scripts of lectures given by Hazrat Pir discusses his teaching as it relates to the history of Sufism, peace, wisdom, knowledge, healing, meditation, love, prayer, balance, and alchemy. The author, Hazrat Pir Molana Salaheddin Ali Nader Shah Angha, is the forty-second master of Maktab Tarighat Oveyssi Shahmaghsoudi *(School of Islamic Sufism)*, a school that traces its lineage back to the very advent of Islam in the seventh century A.D. While Hazrat Pir's lectures are faithful to the tradition which produced him and which he now guides, they also reflect the mark he has made on that tradition. Raised and trained in the esoteric tradition of Sufism and educated in the West, Hazrat Pir is exceptionally sensitive to the modern world. Accomplished in the disciplines of religion, science, philosophy and poetry, and trained by his father, Molana Hazrat Shah Maghsoud Sadegh Angha (Professor Angha), himself a great master of Sufism and an advanced physicist, Hazrat Pir has, from a very young age developed not only a perceptive and accomplished mind, but also an expansive spirit.

Our desire to transform the world, he teaches, must begin with a transformation of "i" into "I", the true Self. To the Sufi, this necessitates a dialogue between heart and mind. What Westerners call internal learning, or self-knowledge is, to the Sufi, more like a glorified "i" short of a transformation into Self. For example, Hazrat Pir teaches that drug addiction, the scourge of modern society, will elude well-meaning people's attempts to eradicate it, until they understand how to heal the mind of its addiction, and discover the stable "I". To heal the mind of its addiction, one must acknowledge that God, and not the ego is at the center of the "I". Only then is one capable of living a healthy and balanced life.

A serious scrutiny of Hazrat Pir's example would serve the purpose of welcoming a science of mind that may well complement the existing one in the West. Islam is much in the news these days and concerned people want to know more about a culture that is at once alien and familiar — as familiar as the lines from the *Holy Qur'an,* "I am closer to you than your jugular vein." Most Westerners would not have ever read these words unless they were familiar with a poem of the same name by French writer James Sacré. Yet there is a certain basic sanity about those words rooted in a deeper source than that of the creative ego. Heirs of the Greek tradition, the West is only beginning to realize why the heart of Islam seems so close — it has always been there, part of its world, part of its culture, part of its "I" from the beginning.

So it seems fitting that on American soil, a nation founded on the spirit of exploration and discovery, Hazrat Pir has designed and built a memorial in memory of his teacher and father, Professor Angha. In three dimensions, near Novato, California stands a wonderful metaphor for 1400 years of spiritual labor and the integration of the human being's consciousness. There in architecture and here in words on the page, Hazrat Pir encourages the seeker to submit to his or her own metamorphosis and flower like the art of the memorial through the integration of Self, through integrity to the final union with God.

Sufism
and
Peace

*In the Name of God,
Most Gracious, Most Merciful*

> There is another way of action and belief — one not bound to custom, tradition, race, culture, personal or social ideologies — yet capable of changing the course of human destiny.

*P*eace and human rights — these are words which create strong emotional feelings in everyone. But what do they really mean? How much of the meaning is known to those who use these words so frequently? And how much of the meaning is known to those who listen to these promises of peace and human rights?

When communication is based on "unknowns", "knowns" cannot be obtained, and positive and effective results cannot be realized. Can you give someone something you yourself do not have? How can you give, when you don't know what it is that you are giving? How can you define something when you don't know what it is?

Wasn't it only a few years ago that Yasser Arafat was considered a terrorist? What changed within these few years?

Who had called him a terrorist, and who calls him a peacemaker now? Who sets the criteria? What is the measure with which the criteria is set? Aren't these questions that should be raised in the mind of any thoughtful and rational human being before making decisions?

Dreaming of peace is not peace!

Everyone speaks of peace and yet there is no peace. Everyone wants peace and yet there is no peace. Each human being's innate urge is to live in peace, and yet people do not cease to fight, kill and destroy.

We do not have true peace or real human rights today. Have we ever had them in the history of humanity? It is said that peace prevailed at the time of the *Pax Romana*. What we have had since recorded time are ever constant disputes, confrontations, conflicts and wars. Humanity's state has been one of constant agitation, uncertainty, hardship and tribulation — along with the erosion of basic human values in society.

The actions of peace groups — whether international or not — result not in the implementation of peace, but rather in the temporary elimination of disputes which, in effect, protects and perpetuates the gains of existing powers. The essential goal of peace has always seemed beyond reach. Even where there is no outright warfare, we find continuing policies of political and economic exploitation, and the prevalence of inequalities.

Economic exploitation takes different forms, and the appearance of "human rights" is proudly advertised by many nations. The ruthless economic competition, the financial manipulations of multinational companies; the sometimes precarious state of worldwide economies and the monetary system; the periodic booms and busts of the world's stock markets; the billions of dollars of debt of numerous nations, both developed and developing; and the shaky economic state of the world's banking system, are all means of exploitation of the weak by the strong.

Peacekeepers, peacemakers, peace organizations, and peace institutes continue to grow in numbers, and yet we do not have peace.

A true understanding of the words "human rights", "personality", and "identity" is crucial in planning for and moving toward peaceful societies. These words are defined according to the cultural, political, and social perspectives of each society. For example, promoting women's rights may be a major political and social concern in one country, in another it may seem irrelevant, and in still another it may go against the grain of the social fabric of that society. If child labor is an acceptable means of survival for one family in one country, in another country it is considered unacceptable and is made illegal. The endless debates we saw over the abortion issue at the recent population conference in Cairo is another example of this dilemma.

Let us take the words "human rights". What is commonly known as "human rights" is a person's right to vote, to free speech, to free press, etc. And, it is generally agreed among "democratic" governments that if these rights are not provided, then people's human rights are violated. If you ask the same people to define what they mean by a human being, they will most probably give you a definition that sums up the human being as the sum total of his or her needs, actions and reactions.

All disciplines — from physical, political, economic, social, psychological, and philosophical viewpoints — have attempted to define the human being. If you look closely at any of the descriptions provided by the above groups, you will see that their definitions are based on their observations of the interaction of the electro-chemical processes of the physical level with the external environment.

Let me take a moment and give a few examples. Scientists run experiments, dissect organs, and perform sophisticated operations, not only to provide effective treatments for problems, but also to present a comprehensive view of the human being. The intricate mechanisms and functions of the human being, which has an average volume of somewhat more than a cubic yard and weighs an average of 170 pounds, are so complex that they exceed the capacity of even the most brilliant and intelligent scientists to totally understand. Numerous specialities and sub-specialities in the field of medicine have evolved to diagnose and provide complete and thorough assessment of various illnesses.

Psychologists and psychoanalysts advance theories based upon their observation of the human being's actions and reactions within society. What psychology originally intended to study was the "psyche" — the word for "soul" in Greek. However, what it actually does study is the behavior of the human being in its various forms of relationships, whereas the study of the "soul", as it was originally intended, has escaped attention.

Researchers in the fields of economics, political science and the social sciences, in general, define the human being as a social unit with needs and dependencies, fulfilling the roles of both producer and consumer in a materialistic society. Theoretical philosophers and social ideologues envision a self-sufficient and prosperous society. They look for a Utopia and construct grand schemes to realize the "ideal society" where order is based upon total obedience to a social system.

If we take any of the above definitions of the human being, and put them next to any of the human rights categories mentioned earlier, we will see that what is spoken of is actually "people's rights" and not "human rights". You are probably wondering what I mean by this. Let me explain it in this manner.

The most fundamental principle in Sufism is, unless a subject is completely known, its benefits and, ultimately, the necessity to make effective plans for its implementation, can never be realized. This principle is applied to knowing the human being, to knowing peace, and to knowing human rights — and knowing one of these completely is to know them all.

Let us take a comprehensive look at the human being. The cause and motive for all movements toward war and peace, the ultimate judge of all things, the repository of all societal strengths as well as weaknesses — is that moving, complex creature called the "human being". The human being is endowed with physical and mental powers, with mind, reason, emotions, imagination and will. Furthermore, the human is the result of millions of years of evolutionary development.

The human being's different dimensions, which are among the wonders of existence, have extensive relationships with both their internal and external environments. The human being in its limited physical state, confined within the dimensions of space, time and place, is also endowed with other attributes which have not received sufficient attention. The resulting human being is not only a synthesis of all these functions, but is also a repository of embedded knowledge.

Just as precious diamonds do not dissolve into the dirt of swamps, and the running veins of pure gold keep their luminosity within the heart of the earth and are loath to mix with the brittle soil in mines, so does the human being bear a distinctive attribute in its earthly, natural being, which is also luminous and has a separate life to undertake. The human being is of earth, but is not mortal. And in the midst of the darkness of nature, the human essence remains unswerving and constant.

This is the dimension that distinguishes the human being from other creatures. In the teachings of Islam, the true identity of the human being is equated with the Divine, as proclaimed by the words, *"la-illaha-illa'llah"* — there is no other but God. And the Holy Prophet Muhammad (peace and blessings upon him) has said, "Whoever cognizes the true self, has cognized God." The true rank of the human being exceeds any definitions provided by the various disciplines mentioned earlier.

In other words, the true human right of each person is the realization of his or her rank as created in the image of God. To understand this statement, we must know and understand the most vital urges of the human being, and know how these urges are translated and expressed through its multi-operative levels.

Let us take this example first. One of the most fundamental needs of the human being is survival. Some may call it self-preservation. Why is there such a need, where does it come from, and how can it be properly understood? On the natural physical level, this urge is translated to mean that the human being will do everything in its power to live, much like other living entities in the world. Therefore, it seeks food, shelter, etc. in order to survive. Reproduction is generally seen as an extension of the need to survive. Therefore, all human activities are geared first towards the protection of this level of existence — feeding, clothing, and protecting the physical body.

However, we see that even when these needs are met, people are not satisfied. The urge to survive takes on a new dimension. If today, bread and water are seen as enough for survival, tomorrow they will be replaced by bread and cheese, the next day by steak and wine, and so on. If today, a roof over the head is sufficient, tomorrow it will be a house, the next day a mansion, and so on. The ones who have more, want more. The ones who do not are pushed further and further into the mere survival mode.

Aggression, greed, oppression, etc. are linked to the human being's identification with earthly life. Fame, wealth, credibility, worldliness, scholarship, and power, are methods through which people are classified and ranked. Therefore, people's identity becomes dependent upon the various social, political, economic, and educational systems whose standards have already been pre-determined by their societies and cultures. Moreover, people begin to adopt and adapt these pre-determined measures as standards after which they model their personalities. Since identities and personalities become associated with worldly accomplishments, people strive to accumulate more wealth, more power, more fame, and so on. To maintain their power, the aggressors continue to oppress, and the oppressed grow in numbers.

Meanwhile, each human being wants to live in peace. The more people engage in worldly pursuits, the more disquiet they become. The affluent and the needy both search for peace. The oppressor and the oppressed both search for methods to numb their disquiet, through lavish lifestyles, alcohol, drugs, violence, or the hope of revenge, while masses of the ignorant are easily led astray by placing all their worries in a blind faith that promises a peaceful and permanent repose in heaven as a reward for their good deeds. In summary, since the human being sees its survival and identity to be dependent on the physical world — whether physically, emotionally, or socially — its appetite for the world becomes insatiable. You can apply this principle to all levels of interaction in society. You can apply it to the smallest unit — the family, or to the largest — the world community. You can see relationships, partnerships, friendships, marriages, come together and fall apart, because the personalities and identities people fabricate for themselves are based upon the standards set by their societies, all arising from the unknown roots of the urge to survive.

If you pay close attention to the physiological system of the human being, you will see that in order to survive, each cell absorbs, assimilates and repels. This is the law governing all living organisms. If it does not repel, but simply gathers and accumulates, imbalance will occur and it will not survive.

As long as human beings interact only from their earthly level of human attachments and needs, greed, injustice, enmity, and inequality will continue to prevail. The instructions of all the Prophets, and especially those of the Prophet Muhammad (peace and blessings upon him) are intended to guide human beings to know their reality, so they may live in balance, peace, and know their eternity. If human beings discover their eternity, their urge for survival will be fulfilled. The fear of death will no longer press them toward seeking earthly fulfillment, which ultimately leads to imbalance and destruction. Neither will they accept false identities and personalities. They will know that their reality is not bounded by the pre-fabricated structures dictated by society.

Therefore, what is commonly referred to as "human rights" should be corrected to say, "people's rights". Yes, society, government, organizations, institutions, etc. can make provisions to improve the standards of living of people. But human rights cannot be forced upon people. Human rights can only be attained through education. If each person is trained to know his or her reality — the true human personality and dignity — can anyone add or take anything away from it? Can dictatorships exist? Can aggression and exploitation exist? Will the result of such a system of training not bring about peace and democracy?

Democracy cannot be forced upon people. It must arise from the people and be sustained by the people, so that it may grow and become strong. It was only last month that the U.S. decided to invade Haiti to re-establish democracy. Anything which is forced upon people will not endure, for the foundation and structure will not be there to provide the necessary support.

The simplest and most general definition for society is that of a system consisting of its people and their behaviors. If we look at any level of contemporary society, we will see that peace does not exist. We see love turn to hatred, partnerships turn to feuds, families dismantled.

Furthermore, if we look at the statistics of suicide, murder, rape, child abuse, domestic violence, and incest, we cannot help but stop and note that there must be something wrong. People turn to food, drugs, alcohol to numb their restlessness and anxieties. Addiction has reached children in the primary grades, and yet educators refuse to look at the situation from a different perspective.

Educational systems should be revised, so children can be effectively educated to know their true human right, their true personality and identity. The system of education should provide a conducive environment where the talents and abilities of children will be developed, so children can realize their true self-worth and stand on their own strength. If children are trained from this perspective, they will not be drawn into the many addictive and destructive patterns of behavior that dominates the lives of the adults, and plagues societies around the world.

I believe it is time that world leaders, educators, and researchers take a good look at the result of their past efforts; put aside partisanship, prejudice, and narrow-mindedness, and change the existing educational system. Unless these changes are made and future generations are trained to know their true human right, there will be no hope for peace, democracy and survival.

We must not think that we need to undertake monumental and intricate projects to attain this goal. It is my opinion that instead of persisting in trying to design and implement an illusory idea known as society, thinkers and leaders should put their efforts towards providing the means by which individuals can be guided to know their true values. The resulting society will then enjoy prosperity, happiness and equality. If each human being is trained to develop all inherent talents and abilities, they will be able to stand against baselesss and unfounded ideas at any cost. They shall know the true meaning of "prosperity for human society," and have sound, constructive ideas and action.

Sufism is the method of instruction of all the Holy Prophets, and the way to introduce each person individually to his or her inherent values and true personality. Sufism, in its teachings, is the educational method through which the human being is reconciled with the heavenly kingdom. The human being is, therefore, trained to develop all creative abilities so that he or she may benefit from all the resources provided by nature, and live in peace, knowledge and justice.

Unless organizations which serve as innovators for social and educational change discover a constant spiritual measure, then such disparate and changeable factors as prejudice and differences in attitudes will not be eliminated. The more we strive toward this goal with all existing resources —natural, material, and above all, human — the sooner we shall reach tangible results and the sooner will the foundation for a unified and stable social system, based upon true human values and relationships, be implemented.

To summarize, the happiness and prosperity that humanity has envisioned and aspired to will prevail only when all individuals benefit from a state of spiritual well-being. A successful human society is attained through the outward and inward harmony of each of its members, and their harmonious existence in a unified system. Without achieving this, all international laws and agreements, and all organizations which use the term "peace" as a concept without its true realization, will fail in creating a prosperous and peaceful society with existing methods.

To arrive at a comprehensive understanding of the human being requires that we distinguish between "real peace" and "pre-fabricated peace", between "human rights", and "people's rights", and between "life" and "living". What system can be more powerful than a society where people have recognized their true human dignity and human right? Can anything but peace prevail in such a society?

In closing, let me quote you a verse from the *Holy Qur'an (50:6)*:

> Why don't you look beyond, at the sky,
> and see how we have set it in place,
> and adorned it without flaw.

If existence can create such perfection, with balance and harmony, then surely we do not need to look very far to find the same perfection, balance and harmony.

Genealogy of Maktab Tarighat Oveyssi Shahmaghsoudi
(School of Islamic Sufism)®

Prophet Mohammad
Imam Ali
Hazrat Oveys Gharani*
Hazrat Salman Farsi
Hazrat Habib-ibn Salim Ra'i
Hazrat Soltan Ebrahim Adham
Hazrat Abu Ali Shaqiq al-Balkhi
Hazrat Sheikh Abu Torab Nakhshabi
Hazrat Sheikh Abi Amr al-Istakhri
Hazrat Abu Ja'far Hazza
Hazrat Sheikh Kabir Abu Abdollah Mohammad-ibn Khafif Shirazi
Hazrat Sheikh Hossein Akkar
Hazrat Sheikh Morshed Abu-Isshaq Shahriar Kazerouni
Hazrat Khatib Abolfath Abdolkarim
Hazrat Ali-ibn Hassan Basri
Hazrat Serajeddin Abolfath Mahmoud-ibn Mahmoudi Sabouni Beyzavi
Hazrat Sheikh Abu Abdollah Rouzbehan Baghli Shirazi
Hazrat Sheikh Najmeddin Tamat-al Kobra Khivaghi
Hazrat Sheikh Ali Lala Ghaznavi
Hazrat Sheikh Ahmad Zaker Jowzeghani
Hazrat Noureddin Abdolrahman Esfarayeni
Hazrat Sheikh Alaoddowleh Semnani
Hazrat Mahmoud Mazdaghani
Hazrat Amir Seyyed Ali Hamedani
Hazrat Sheikh Ahmad Khatlani
Hazrat Seyyed Mohammad Abdollah Ghatifi al-Hasavi Nourbakhsh
Hazrat Shah Ghassem Feyzbakhsh
Hazrat Hossein Abarghoui Janbakhsh
Hazrat Darvish Malek Ali Joveyni
Hazrat Darvish Ali Sodeyri
Hazrat Darvish Kamaleddin Sodeyri
Hazrat Darvish Mohammad Mozaheb Karandehi (Pir Palandouz)
Hazrat Mir Mohammad Mo'men Sodeyri Sabzevari
Hazrat Mir Mohammad Taghi Shahi Mashhadi
Hazrat Mir Mozaffar Ali
Hazrat Mir Mohammad Ali
Hazrat Seyyed Shamseddin Mohammad
Hazrat Seyyed Abdolvahab Naini
Hazrat Haj Mohammad Hassan Kouzekanani
Hazrat Agha Abdolghader Jahromi
Hazrat Jalaleddin Ali Mir Abolfazl Angha
Hazrat Mir Ghotbeddin Mohammad Angha
Hazrat Molana Shah Maghsoud Sadegh Angha
Hazrat Salaheddin Ali Nader Shah Angha

The conventional Arabic transliteration is Uways al-Qarani